S0-AGA-486

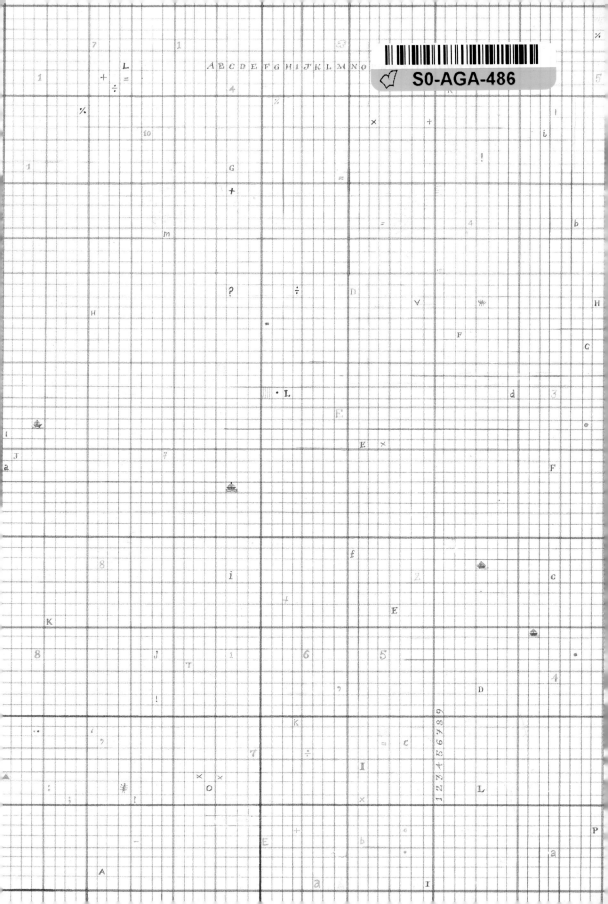

GROWING UP AND OTHER VICES

FOR K·H·P

GROWING UP
AND OTHER VICES

SARA MIDDA

JONATHAN CAPE
London

FIRST PUBLISHED 1994

1 3 5 7 9 10 8 6 4 2

© Sara Midda 1994

Sara Midda has asserted her right under
the Copyright, Designs and Patents Act 1988
to be identified as the author of this work

First published in the United Kingdom in 1994 by
Jonathan Cape Limited
Random House, 20 Vauxhall Bridge Road , London SW1 2SA

Random House UK Limited Reg. No. 954009

A CIP catalogue record for this book
is available from the British Library

ISBN 0 224 03714 5

Printed in Singapore

Adults have an amazing
ability for underestimating the strength of a child's emotions.

INDIGNITIES

COMMUNAL BATHING

INVASION OF PRIVACY

SKIN HAVING TO BE REINFORCED

LOSS OF CONSTANT FOOD SUPPLY

OBLIGATION TO BE SOCIABLE

RESTRICTED SLEEP

UNCOMFORTABLE TRANSPORT

NOISE

IRRITATION OF BABY TALK

TEETHING

LITTLE UNDISTURBED THINKING TIME

MOBILITY

NOT EVERYTHING IS EDIBLE

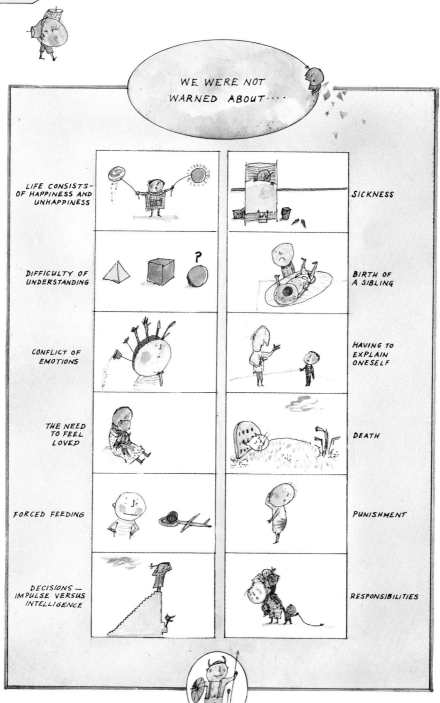

WE WERE NOT WARNED ABOUT····

LIFE CONSISTS— OF HAPPINESS AND UNHAPPINESS

SICKNESS

DIFFICULTY OF UNDERSTANDING

BIRTH OF A SIBLING

CONFLICT OF EMOTIONS

HAVING TO EXPLAIN ONESELF

THE NEED TO FEEL LOVED

DEATH

FORCED FEEDING

PUNISHMENT

DECISIONS — IMPULSE VERSUS INTELLIGENCE

RESPONSIBILITIES

BEHAVIOUR TOWARDS VARIOUS CREATURES.

NEVER

Offend a cat

Incarcerate blackbirds

Argue with a rhinoceros

Bewilder a bumble-bee

Confuse a fish

Bite dogs

Deprive a centipede of its boots

Turn horses into zebras

Misuse a camel

Evict a mollusc

Unwind a pig's tail

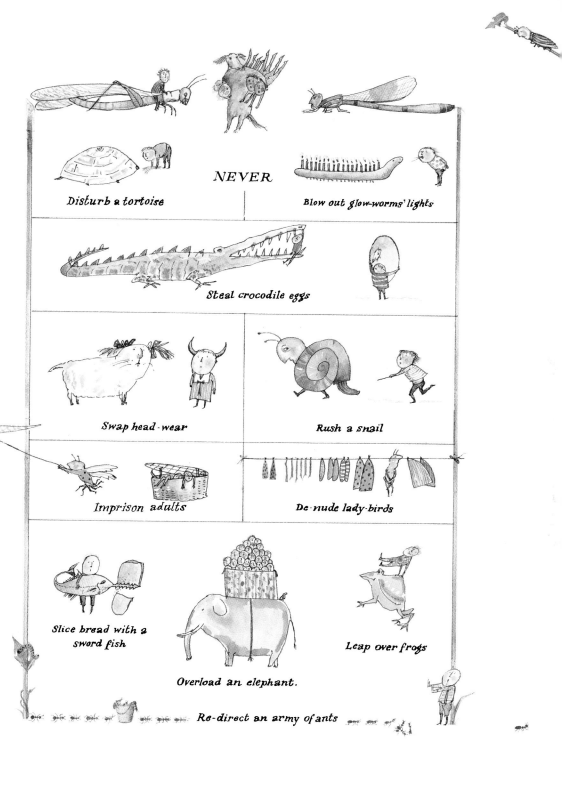

NEVER

Disturb a tortoise

Blow out glow-worms' lights

Steal crocodile eggs

Swap head-wear

Rush a snail

Imprison adults

De-nude lady-birds

Slice bread with a
sword fish

Overload an elephant.

Leap over frogs

Re-direct an army of ants

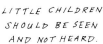

LITTLE CHILDREN
SHOULD BE SEEN
AND NOT HEARD.

OR NOT SEEN

NOR HEARD

THIS LEADS TO —

Secrets

Confused emotions

Doubts

Fears

Uncertainty

Bad memories

Refusal to talk

Dependency

Timidity

Inhibitions

Moods

Daydreams

THINGS YOU ARE **SUPPOSED** TO GROW OUT OF · · · ·

SHYNESS	BLUSHING	BASHFULNESS	ACNE
BURPING	BEING IGNORED	PUPPY FAT	UNTIDINESS
UNCONTROLLABLE GIGGLES	FEAR OF OPPOSITE SEX	SULKING	NAIL BITING
HATRED OF SPINACH	STARING	NOSE PICKING	AVERSION TO BRUSHES
SELFISHNESS	STEALING APPLES	PULLING OUT TONGUE	THUMB SUCKING
THROWING TANTRUMS	EMBARRASSED BY PARENTS	DISTRESSED BY FRECKLES	DISLIKE OF HAIR COLOUR

OLD AGE

22
21
20
19
18
17
16 MATURITY
15
14
13
12
11
10
9
8
7
6
5
4
3
2
1
0

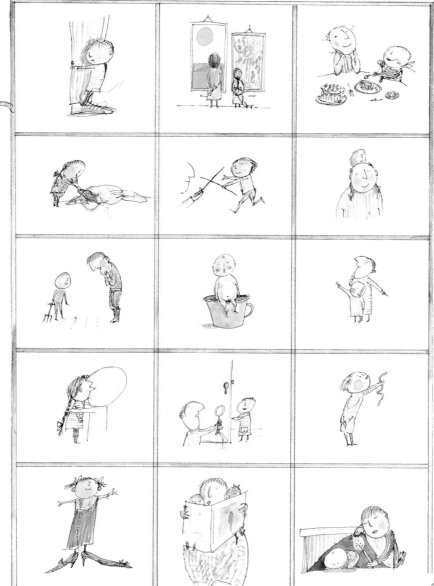

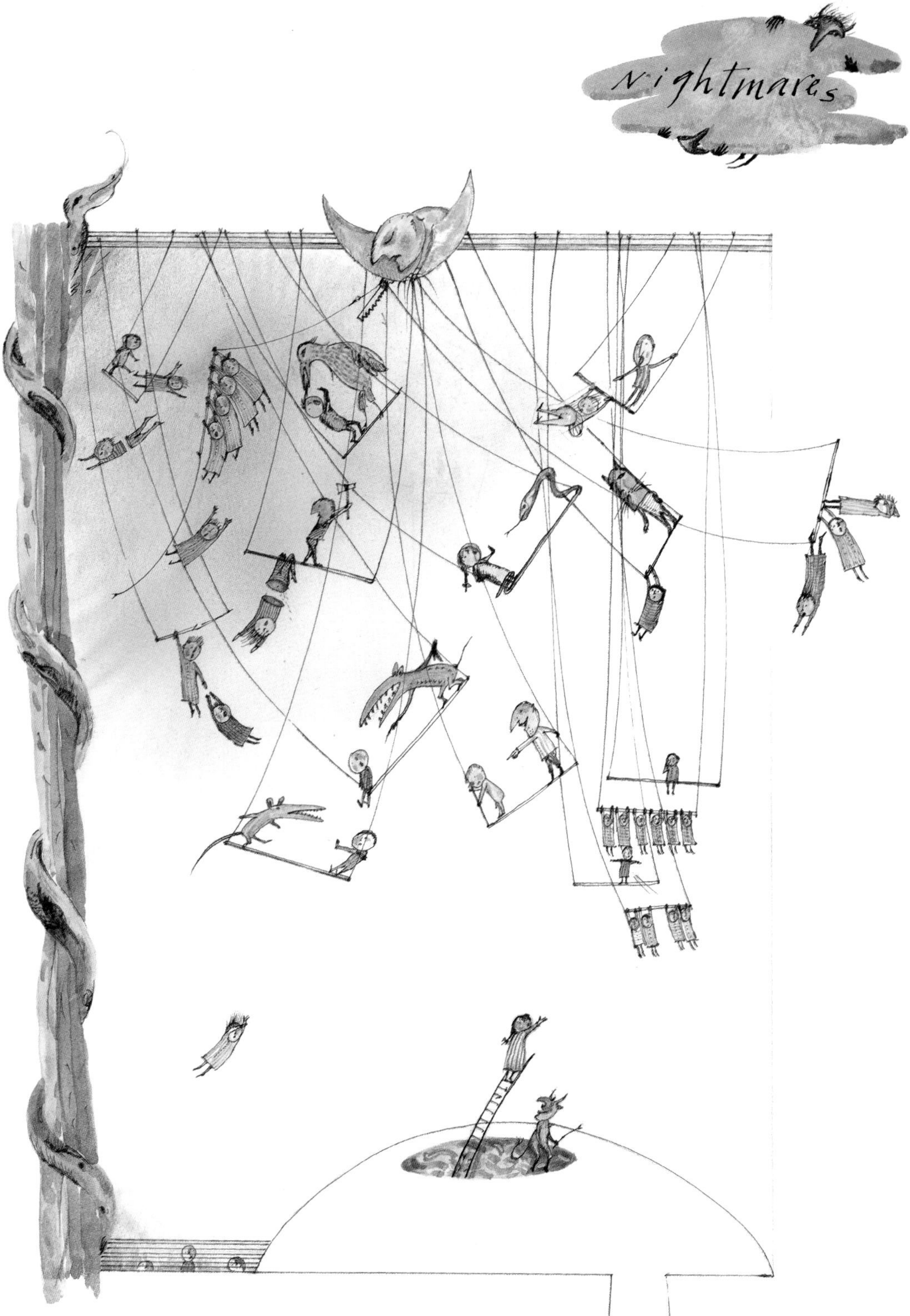
nightmares

TABLE MANNERS

If you stuff too much into your mouth, you may explode.

De capitate eggs swiftly. Poke neither finger nor tongue into them.

Do not rummage through the dish to find the tastiest morsel for yourself.

Spitting out food is rude, as is spitting on food to mark it as yours.

Do not begin eating — until invited.

Eating with long teeth shows a distate of meal.

Concentrate very hard to avoid farting.

Never treat food disrespectfuly

On discovering something disgusting — hide it.

Do come to the table improperly Not dressed

A pigeon pie   Cut it   Take it   Peep into it   Prepare to eat . . . .

ON MATTERS CONCERNING THE STOMACH

Wash hands before meals

Remove sticky fingers.

Never show contents of mouth to fellow diners.

It is important to know when to stop eating.

Do not scratch. Hands on table avoids suspicion.

none of this, no onions, no garlic, n

INCORRECT BEHAVIOUR

THE PERFECT DINER

INCORRECT BEHAVIOUR

Food should not be played with, nor used as ammunition.

Aerating causes belching

Do not hold cutlery like sticks

Be sure to ask permission before getting down from table.

THE FORK

Supposedly useful implement for eating peas.

THE SPOON, Can be used instead of cupped hands.

THE KNIFE

Avoid contact between knife and round object.

CHILD AS VICTIM

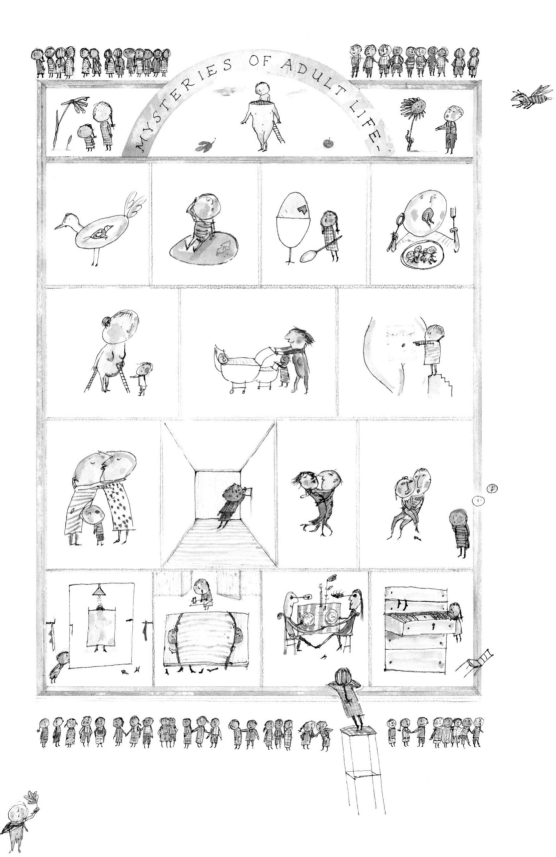

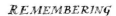

First bicycle
Wild blackberries. Old apple trees. Primroses.
Smell of baking. Fresh grass
Shuffling through autumn leaves
Picnics – Hard-boiled eggs, tickling of grass + insects
Sand and bread in one's mouth.
Pebbles under water
Not being chosen (for a team)
Digging up old pottery
A rocking horse envied
Walking on pebbles
Rock pools and limpets
Swing in the beech tree
Cold, marbled knees.
Penknife – whittling sticks

Tame fly
Rabbit's burial
First paints, brushes and pencils
Being taken seriously
Trying to whistle
Kaleidoscope

Chocolate cake
Collecting lupin seeds
Betrayal by an adult
Surgery on a bear
Damming streams
Blackbird's song
Picking sweet peas
The drawer of cotton reels
Secret codes

Building cities
Shucking peas
Rough woollen shorts
Secret hiding place.
Skin on rice pudding
Caterpillars, worms
Hidden book
First conker of autumn

Conversation with adult

First argument.

First friend

Fly
Concentrate
Float
Write with a pen
Wriggle ears
Spell

Stand baths
Do handstands
Blow bubble gum
Remember dates

Sit up straight
Make a fire with two sticks
Peel oranges

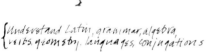

→ {Understand Latin, grammar, algebra, verbs, geometry, languages, conjugations

Drink milk
Eat yolk of fried egg whole.

Sing, dance, be the "Perfect" child
Be restrained when eating liquorice
Separate day dreams from reality
Overcome feelings of failure
Be unafraid of screaming cats
Relate words to images
Be the right age (to be allowed to do things)
Stop fidgeting
Climb down trees
Walk into a room full of people
Grow un-worm eaten radishes

Resist tickling tadpoles
Catch newts
Imagine monsters did not exist

Stop the tide demolishing sand-castles

Explain feelings of anguish

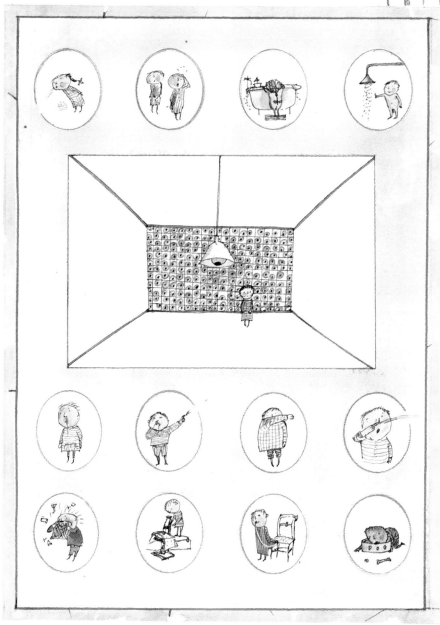

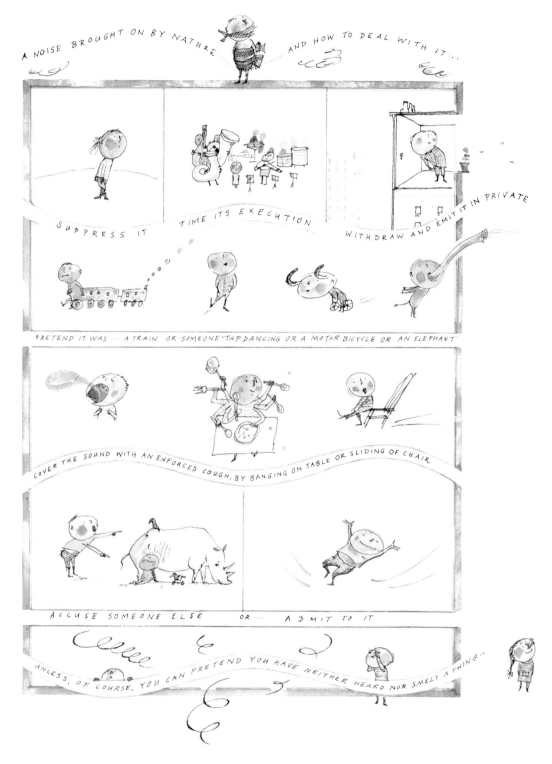

A NOISE BROUGHT ON BY NATURE ... AND HOW TO DEAL WITH IT...

SUPPRESS IT   TIME ITS EXECUTION   WITHDRAW AND EMIT IT IN PRIVATE

PRETEND IT WAS ... A TRAIN OR SOMEONE TAP DANCING OR A MOTOR BICYCLE OR AN ELEPHANT

COVER THE SOUND WITH AN ENFORCED COUGH, BY BANGING ON TABLE OR SLIDING OF CHAIR

ACCUSE SOMEONE ELSE   OR ....   ADMIT TO IT

UNLESS, OF COURSE, YOU CAN PRETEND YOU HAVE NEITHER HEARD NOR SMELT A THING ...

Sibling rivalry

NEVER

Dispose of it	Abandon it	Hide its toys

Embalm it	Take away its food	Infuriate it

Undermine it	Occupy its bed	Try to exchange or send it back.

Little children should be seen and not heard

You are always either too young or too old

Puppet handler

Power sharing

Parental disappointment

It is a wise child knows its own mother

W, V, M, N ?

Aa
Bb
Cc
Dd
Ee
Ff
Gg
Hh
Ii
Jj
Kk
Ll
Mm
Nn
Oo
Pp
Qq
Rr
Ss
Tt
Uu
Vv
Ww
Xx
Yy
Zz

SNEAK

SWOT

CREEP

GOODY-GOODY

TWO FACED

FIBBER

BRAGGER

CHEAT

BULLY

FICKLE

YOU MUST NOT …

Carve on trees

misuse them

or set fire to them.

Stop the rain

Hide too many adults in sand

Repaint the sunset

Get lost in snowstorms

Expect mountains to reply

Interfere with the weather

Hold the ocean upside-down

Investigate seeds' growth

Attempt to re-direct tornadoes

Do not trespass.
The moon is occupied.

Mud should not
be camouflaged as cake

Rise quietly
and do not wake the sun.

Do not
imitate geysers.

It is inadvisable to
expose yourself to the sun

Rearranging rainbows
will confuse

Taming clouds
is dangerous

Horizons should not
be mistaken for tightropes

Never surrender
to shooting stars

Beware of digging
up wild plants

Waves should not
be expected to part

No part of the landscape
should be removed

16 + 1

STEALING	INDIFFERENCE	LYING	ARROGANCE
VIOLENCE	JEALOUSY	DISLOYALTY	GLUTTONY
DESTRUCTIVENESS	INTOLERANCE	SELF - PITY	ENVY
SLOTH	CHEATING	DISHONESTY	CRUELTY

DEADLY SINS

GREED

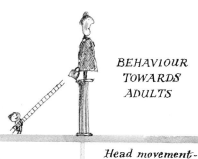

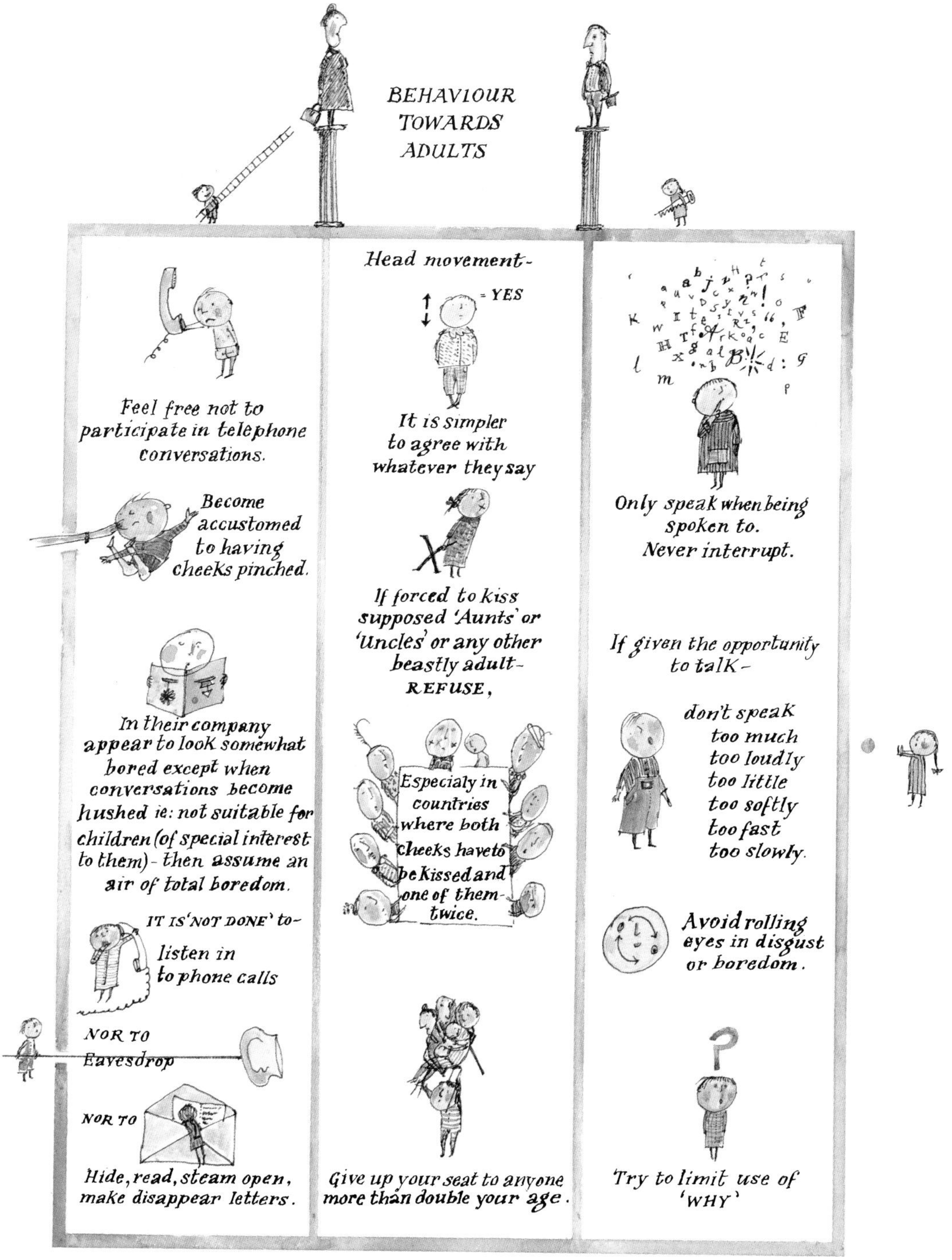

BEHAVIOUR TOWARDS ADULTS
Feel free not to participate in telephone conversations.
Become accustomed to having cheeks pinched.
In their company appear to look somewhat bored except when conversations become hushed ie: not suitable for children (of special interest to them) - then assume an air of total boredom.
IT IS 'NOT DONE' to -
listen in to phone calls
NOR TO
Eavesdrop
NOR TO
Hide, read, steam open, make disappear letters.
Head movement -
= YES
It is simpler to agree with whatever they say
If forced to kiss supposed 'Aunts' or 'Uncles' or any other beastly adult -
REFUSE,
Especialy in countries where both cheeks have to be kissed and one of them twice.
Give up your seat to anyone more than double your age.
Only speak when being spoken to.
Never interrupt.
If given the opportunity to talk -
don't speak
too much
too loudly
too little
too softly
too fast
too slowly.
Avoid rolling eyes in disgust or boredom.
Try to limit use of 'WHY'

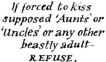

FALL OF THE ADULT

Occurs on realisation
that the Adult is not
perfect.

They do not believe in
our memories.

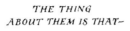

They are illogical

They refuse to believe
children have headaches.

They impose their taste.

They are inconsistent.

They fuss.

They do not allow us to
develop our own judgement.

They confuse us with
bribes and threats.

They have illusions of
omnipotence.

They have a need to
shut one out.

They think 'Because I
say so', is adequate logic.

They try to control
our inner world.

Some even pretend
children do not exist.

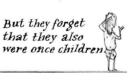

But they forget
that they also
were once children.

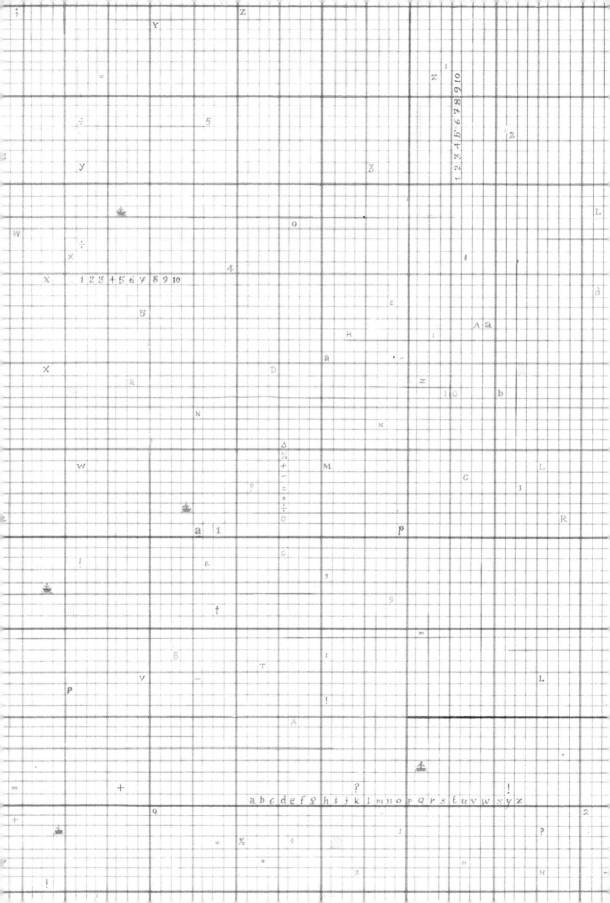